HOW TO DRAW MONSTERS

Learn How to Draw 50 Monsters The Easy Way

Mark Mulle

ISBN-13: 978-1542791175
ISBN-10: 1542791170

Do you want to know how to draw monsters?

This guide will show you how to draw 50 different monsters starting from scratch to its final details. Some of the monsters are easy to draw and some are a little challenging, but as you will discover in the book everything starts from circles and lines. So as long as you can draw circles and lines you'll be able to draw these cute monster characters.

So what are you waiting for?
1. Sharpen your pencil
2. Get your paper
3. Have an eraser too to erase errors and to remove line guides
4. Grab your crayons so you can also color your masterpiece
5. and last of all Have fun!!!

1.

Draw a circular guide for the body of the monster. Put line guides forthe legs, arms and ears.

2.

Draw the circular body of the monster.

3. Draw the legs and the arms. Draw only four fingers for the hands and and three fingers for the feet.

4. Draw two medium circles for the eyes and draw a smaller shaded circle inside the big ones, two small holes for the nose and a big open mouth.

4. Draw leaf like ears, a few pointed teeth and sharp nails.

5. Remove the line guides. Add scales and lines for details.

1.

Draw a circular guide for the body of the monster.
Add another three small circular guide for his eyes.
Add line guides for the legs, arms and tail.

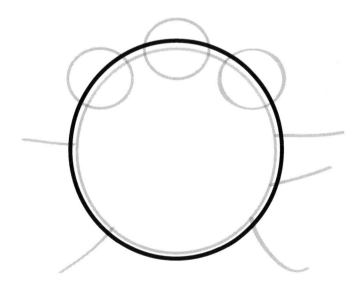

2.

Draw the circular outline of the monster's body.

3.

Draw three eyes at the top of his head.

4.

Create a huge funnel shaped nose with three holes. Draw a big mouth with sharp teeth.

5.

Draw his arms, legs and tail. Draw only three fingers for the hands and feet.

6.

Remove the line guides.

1.

First, draw an oblong guide for the monster's head. Create line guides for the legs, arms and antennae.

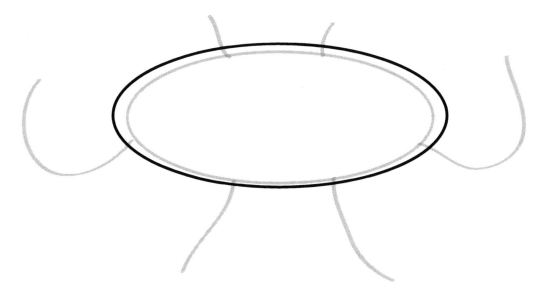

2.

Draw the head of the monster.

3. Draw the legs and arms of the monster.

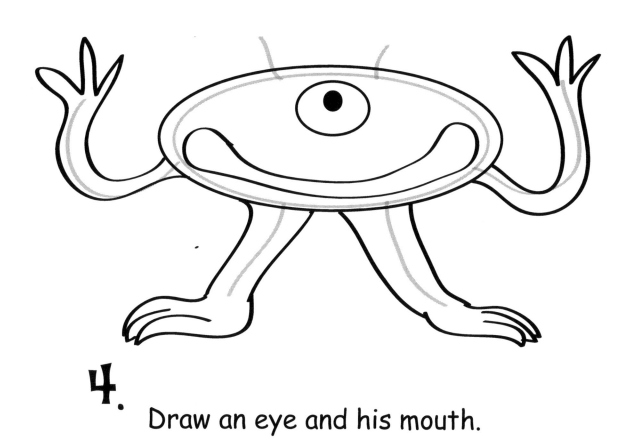

4. Draw an eye and his mouth.

5. Draw the antennae, sharp teeth and nails.

6. Remove the line guides. Add scales and thin lines on its body for details.

1.

First, draw two round guides for the monster's head and body. Create line guides for the legs, arms and tail.

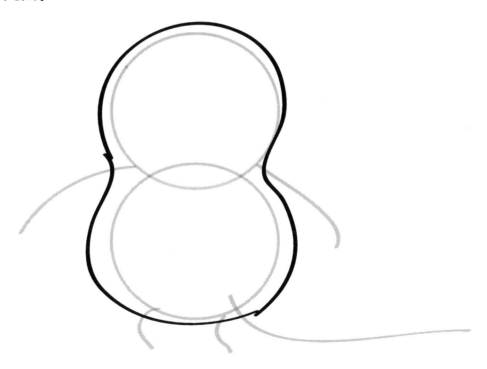

2.

Draw the outline of the monster's head and body.

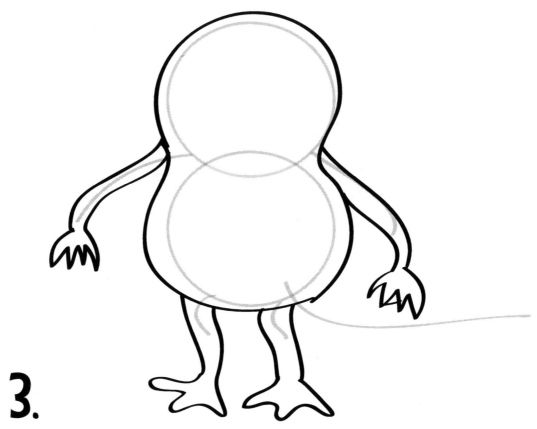

3.

Draw the arms and legs.

4.

Draw the eyes, nose and mouth.

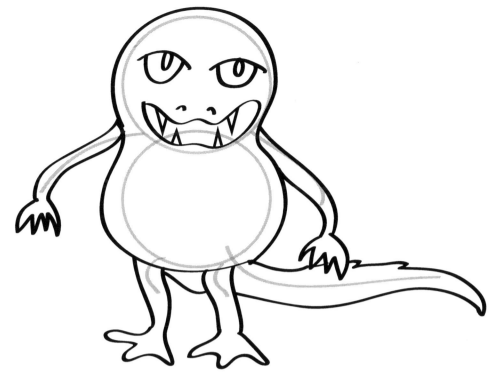

5. Draw its tail and teeth.

6.

Draw a circle in the middle of its body.
Remove the line guides.

1.

Draw a small circular guide for the head of the monster. Create a bigger circular guide for his body. Add line guides for the legs and arms.

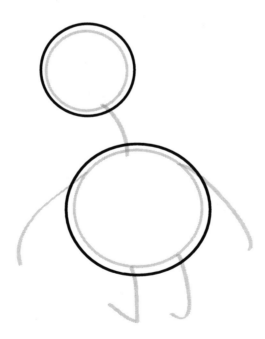

2.

Draw the outline of the monster's head and his body.

3.
Draw the legs and the arms of the monster.

4.
Draw the eye, mouth and teeth.

5.
Draw its neck. Draw parallel horizontal thin lines on it.

6.
Draw a circle in the middle of its body. Remove the line guides.

1.

Draw a circular guide for the body of the monster.
Put line guides for the legs.

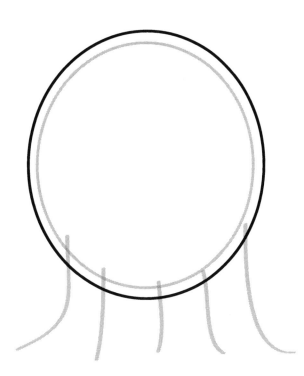

2.

Draw the outline of its body.

3.

Draw the legs of the monster.

4.

Draw its 8 eyes in different sizes.

5.

Draw a thin curve line for its mouth and add a sharp tooth on both of its ends.

6.

Remove the line guides and draw small circles inside the body

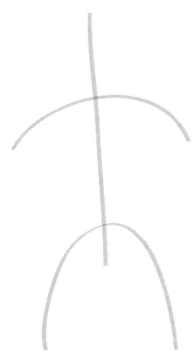

1. Draw line guides for the monster's body, legs and arms.

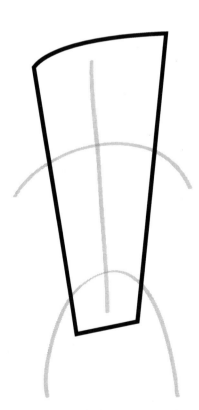

2.

Draw the outline of its body.

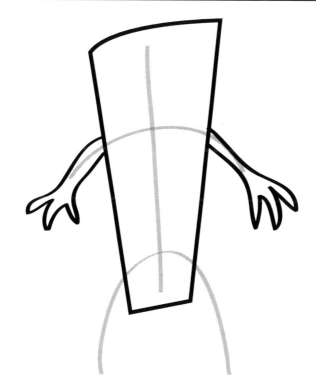

3.

Draw the arms of the monster with three fingers on both hands.

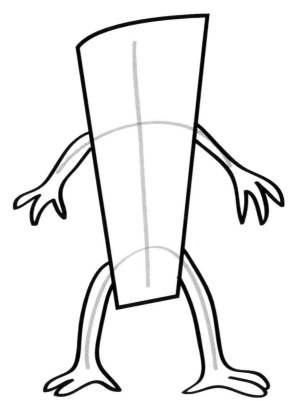

4.

Draw the legs of the monster with three fingers on both feet.

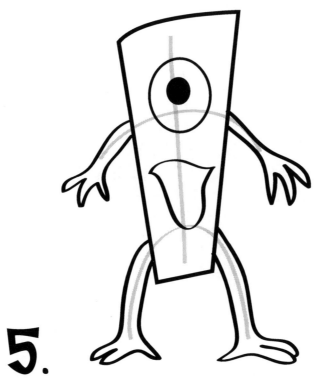

5. Draw its eye and mouth.

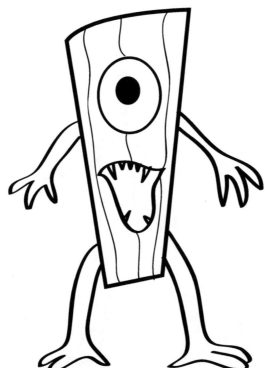

6. Remove the line guides. Draw thin vertical lines on its body to add details.

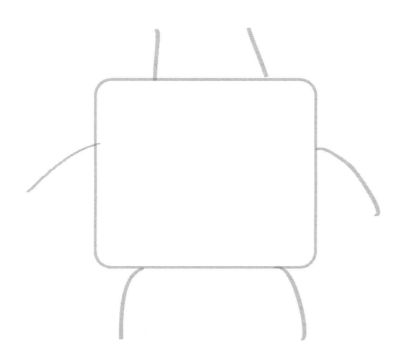

1.

Draw a square guide for the monster's body.
Draw line guides for the legs, arms and horns.

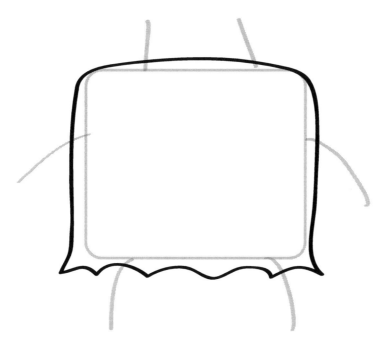

2.

Draw the outline of it's body.

3.

Draw its legs and arms.

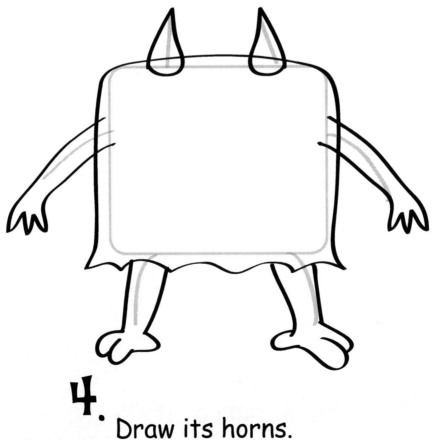

4.

Draw its horns.

5. Draw the eyes, nose and mouth.

6. Draw the teeth. Remove the line guides.

1.

Draw a large round guide for the monster's body. Draw line guides for its legs, too.

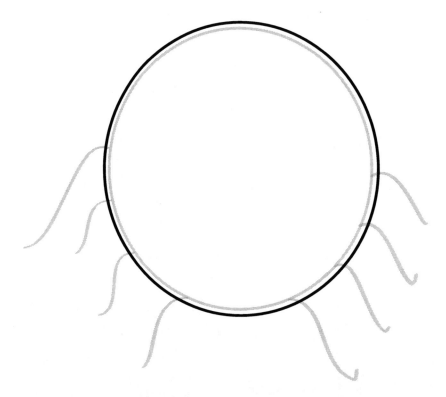

2.

Draw the outline of the body.

3.

Draw the 8 legs of the monster.

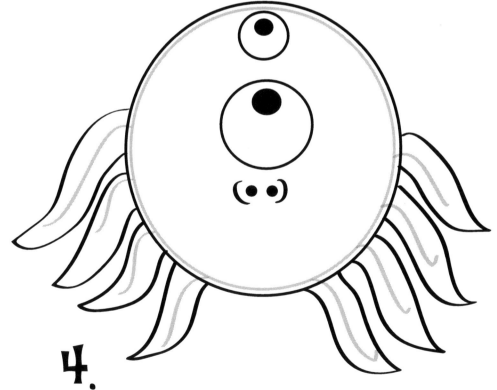

4.

Draw its eyes and nose.

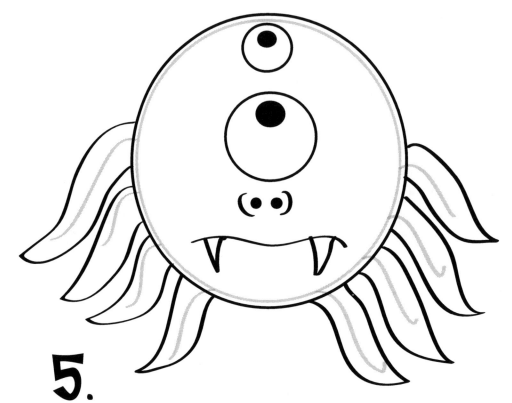

5.

Draw its mouth and teeth.

6.

Remove the line guides. Put small circles and dots all over its body.

1.

Draw a circular guide for the monster's body. Create line guides for his arms and legs.

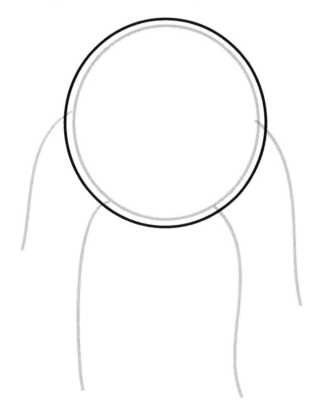

2.

Draw the circular outline of the monster's body.

3. Draw the arms of the monster.

4. Now, draw his long legs.

5. Draw three eyes, nose and mouth.

6. Remove the line guides. Draw some thin line all over the body to add details. Draw scales on his head to make him look more scary.

1. Draw a round guide for the monster's head. Draw another smaller round guide for his body. Create line guides for his legs, arms and ears.

2.

Draw the outline of the monster's head.

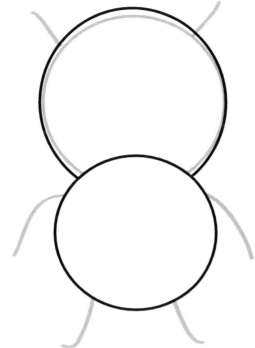

3.

Draw the outline of the monster's body.

4.

Draw the monster's arms and legs.

5. Draw the eyes, nose, mouth, ears and teeth.

6. Remove the line guides. Draw thin lines all over its body to add details. Draw its pointed finger nails.

1.

Draw a big round guide for the monster's body. Draw small round guides for its eyes. Draw line guides for the legs and line guides that connects its body and the eyes.

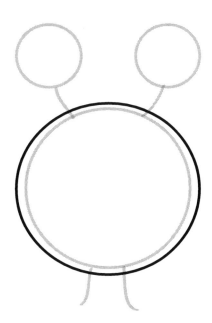

2.

Draw the round outline of the body

3.

Draw the eyes of the monster and the parts that connect the eyes to the body.

4.

Draw the mouth and teeth.

5. Draw the legs of the monster.

6.

Remove the line guides. Draw scales on its body.

1.

Draw a round guide for the monster's body.
Draw line guides for arms, legs and antennae.

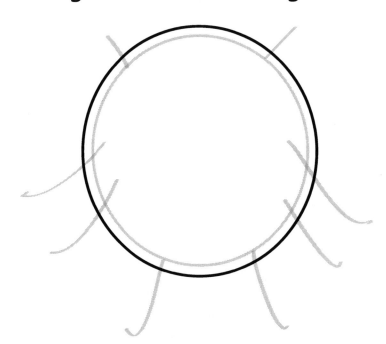

2.

Draw the outline of the monster's body.

3.

Draw the monster's one big eye. Draw a curve line for its mouth and two sharp teeth.

4.

Draw the legs and antennae.

5.

Draw the four arms of the monsters.

6.

Remove the line guides. Draw some thin lines on its body to add details.

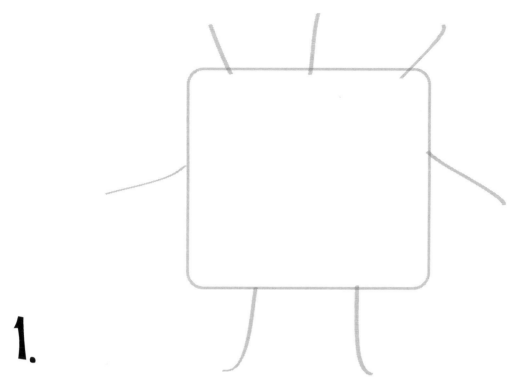

1.

Draw a square guide for the monster's body.
Draw line guides for its legs, arms and horn.

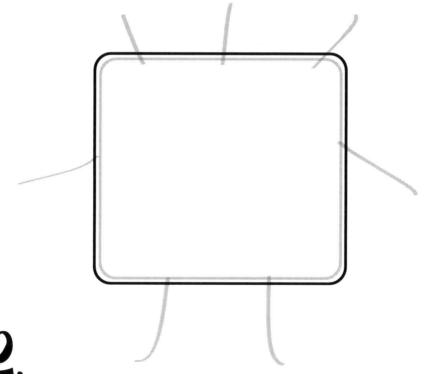

2.

Draw the outline of the body.

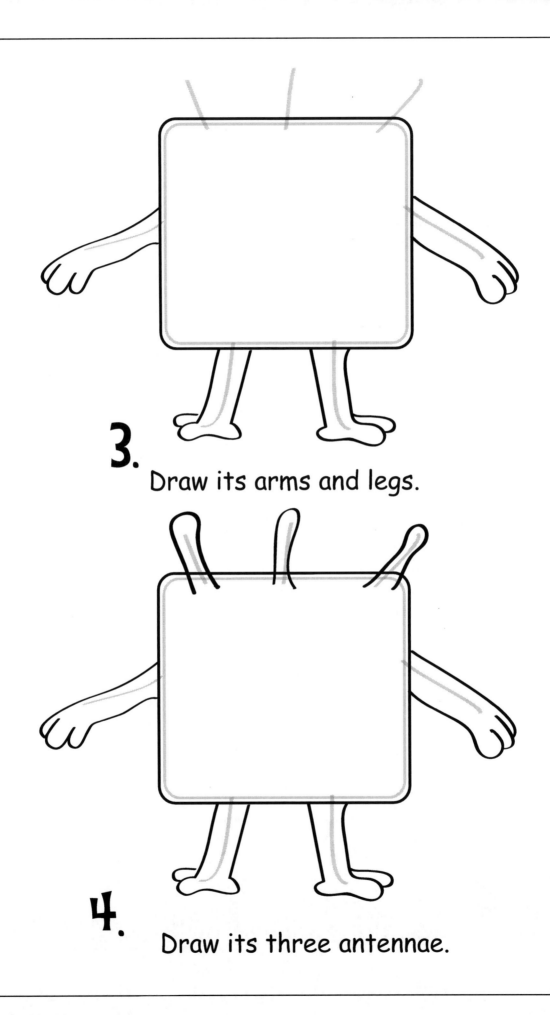

3. Draw its arms and legs.

4. Draw its three antennae.

5.

Draw its three eyes. There should be one big eye in the middle and two smaller eyes on its side. Draw a round mouth, too.

6.

Draw its rectangular teeth. Remove the line guides.

1.

Draw a round guide for the monster's body.
Draw line guides for the legs and the parts where
the eyes are located.

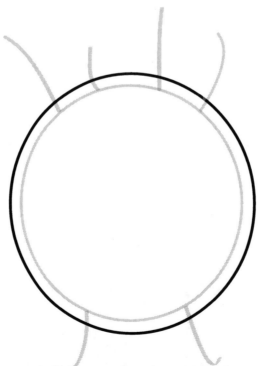

2.

Draw the outline of its body.

3. Draw the monster's legs.

4. Draw the monster's eyes.

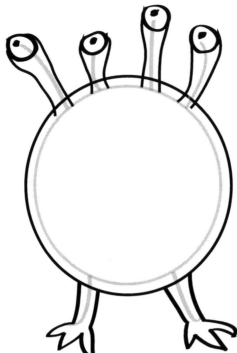

5. Draw tubes that connect the eyes to the monster's body

6. Draw its mouth and teeth. Remove the line guides. Put some thin line for details.

1.

Draw a round guide for the monster's body.
Draw line guides for its legs, arms, ears and horns.

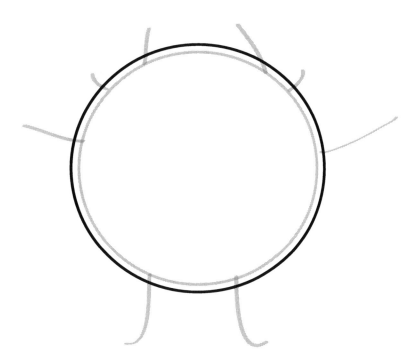

2.

Draw the outline of the monster's body.

3. Draw the monster's legs and arms.

4. Draw the monster's ears and horns.

5. Draw the monster's eyes and mouth.

6. Draw its teeth. Remove the line guides. Draw some small circles and thin lines all over its body for details.

1. Draw a round guide for the monster's body. Draw line guides for its legs, arms and ears.

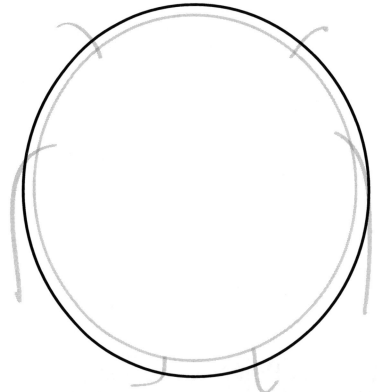

2. Draw the outline of its body.

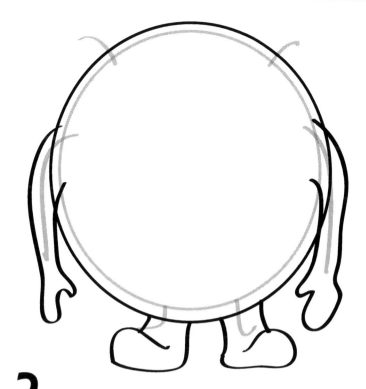

3.

Draw its arms and legs.

4.

Draw its eyes and mouth.

5.

Draw its teeth and ears.

6.

Remove the line guides. Draw small circles all over its body for details.

1.

Draw 3 round guides for the monster's body.
Draw line guides for its legs, arms and horns

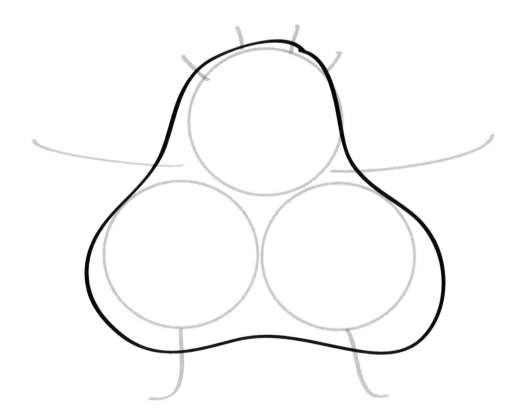

2.

Draw the outline of the monster's body.

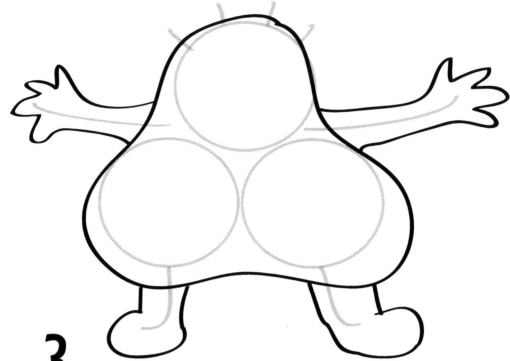

3. Draw its legs and arms.

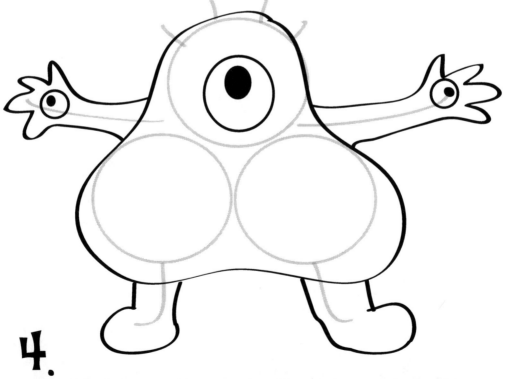

4. Draw its eyes on its head and hands.

5.

Draw its mouth and horns.

6.

Draw its teeth and remove all the line guides.

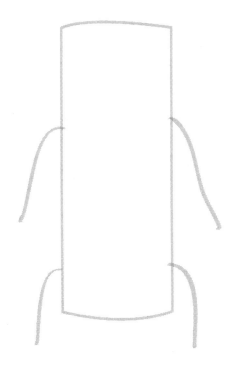

1.

Draw a rectangular guide vertically for the monster's body. Draw line guides for its legs and arms.

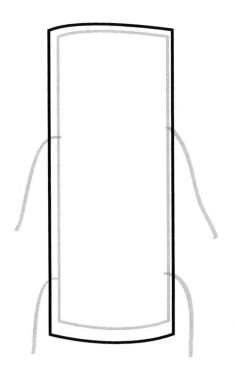

2.

Draw the outline of the monster's body.

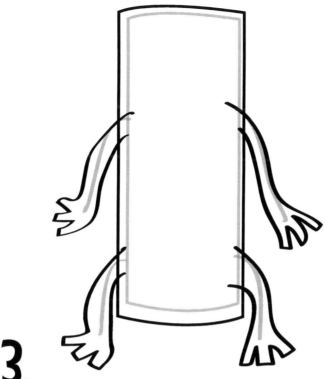

3. Draw its legs and arms.

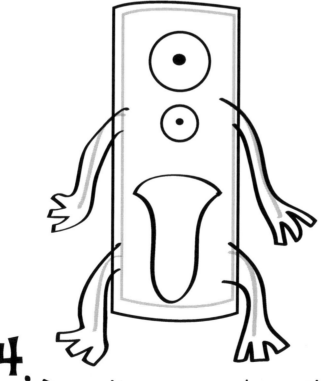

4. Draw its eyes and mouth.

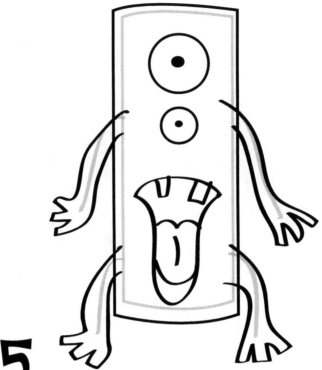

5. Draw its teeth and tongue.

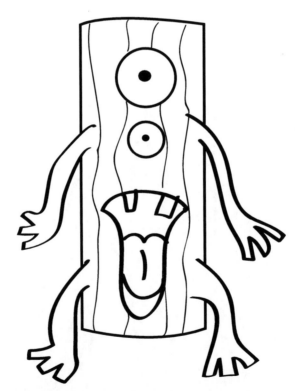

6. Remove the line guides. Draw thin vertical lines all over its body.

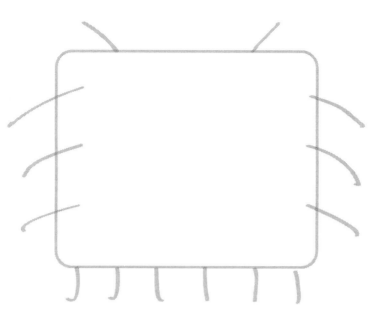

1.

Draw a square guide for the monster's body and line guides for its legs and arms.

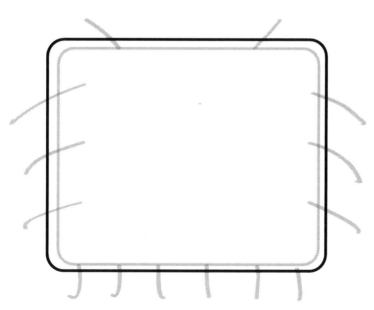

2.

Draw the outline of the monster's body.

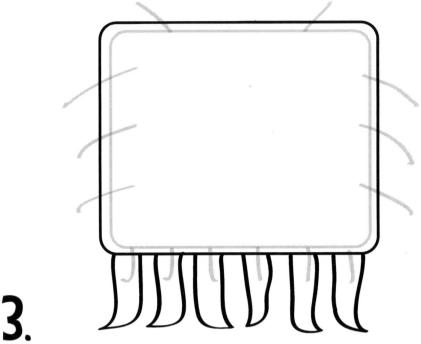

3.

Draw the six legs of the monster.

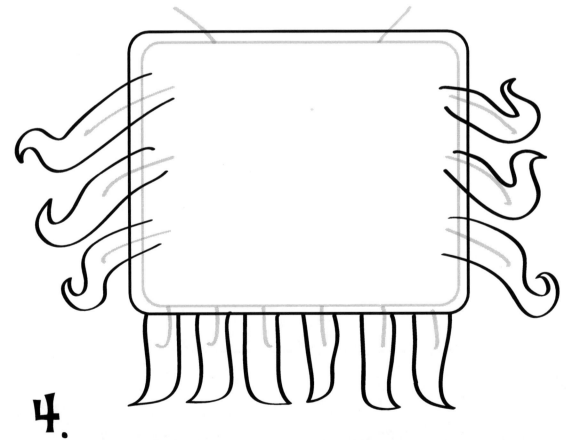

4.

Draw the six arms of the monster.

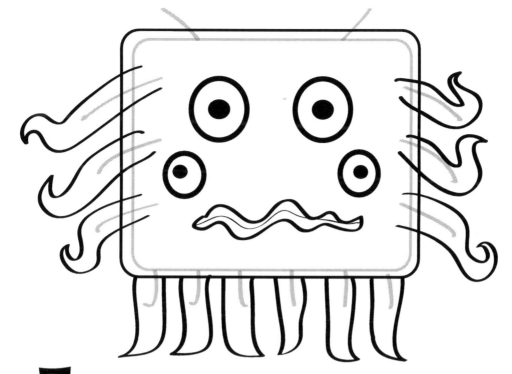

5. Draw its four eyes and mouth.

6. Draw its antennae. Remove the line guides.

1.

Draw a round guide for the monster's body.
Draw line guides for the arms and legs.

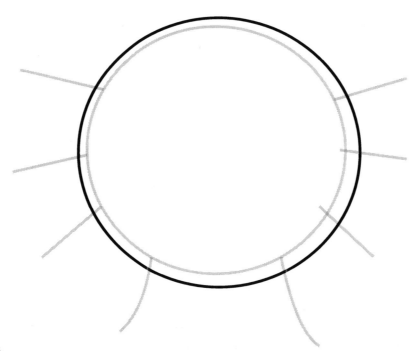

2.

Draw the outline of its body.

3. Draw the legs of the monster.

4. Draw the six arms of the monster.

5.
Draw its eyes and mouth.

6.
Draw its teeth. Remove the line guides.
Draw thin lines and small dots all over
its body for details.

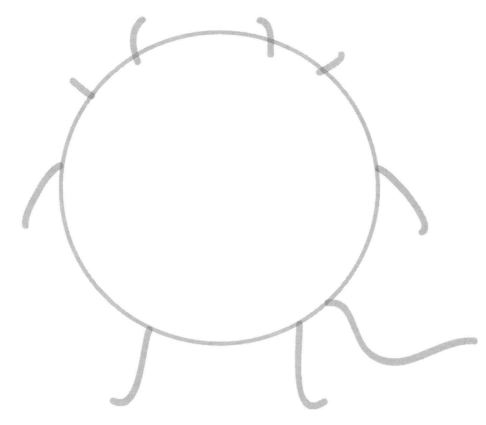

1.

Draw a round guide for the monster's body and line guides for its legs, ear, tail, antennae and arms.

2.

Draw the outline of its body.

3. Draw the legs and arms of the monster.

4. Draw the eyes and mouth of the monster.

5.

Draw its ears and antennae.

6.

Draw its tail and remove the line guides.

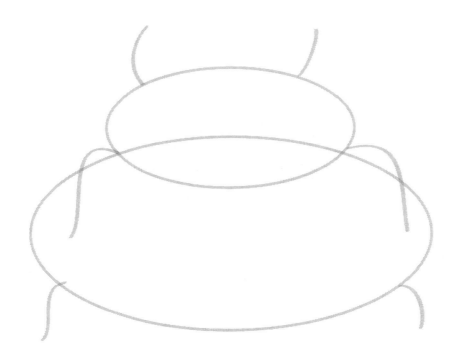

1. Draw round guides for the monster's head and body. Draw line guides for the legs, arms and ears.

2. Draw the outline of the head and the body.

3. Draw the legs and arms of the monster.

4. Draw its eyes and mouth.

5. Draw the ears and teeth.

6. Remove the line guides. Draw small circles of various sizes all over its body.

1.

Draw a round guide for the monster's body.
Draw line guides for the legs, arms and ears.

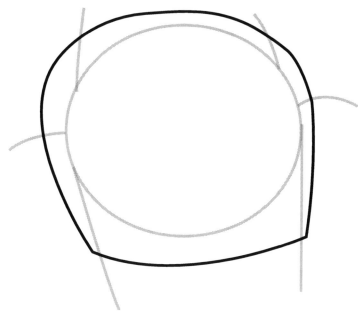

2.

Draw the outline of its body.

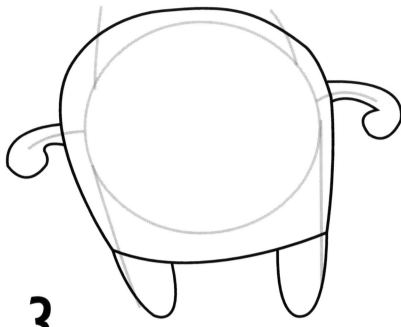

3. Draw its arms and legs.

4. Draw its eyes and ears.

5. Draw its curvy mouth and sharp teeth.

6. Draw horizontal lines on both legs. Remove the line guides.

1.

Draw a round guide for the monster's body. Draw line guides for the legs, arms and antennae.

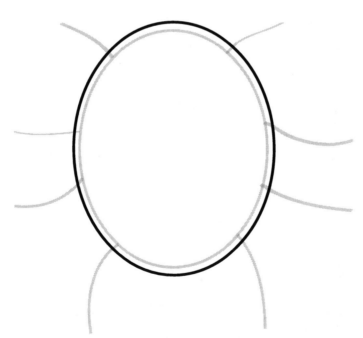

2.

Draw the outline of the monster's body.

3. Draw the legs of the monster.

4. Draw the arms of the monster.

5. Draw a big eye and three little eyes.
Draw its mouth, too.

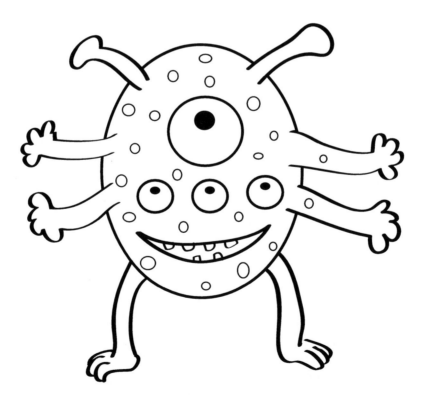

6. Draw its antennae and teeth. Remove the
line guides. Add small circles all over its body.

1. First, draw round guides for the body and lines for the arms, legs and horns.

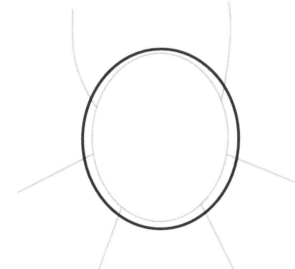

2. Draw the body of the monster.

3.
Draw the arms and legs of the monster.

4.
Draw the horns of the monster.

5.

Draw the eyes of the monster.

6.

Draw the mouth and teeth of the monster. Remove the line guides. Add three dots on its face and curly lines on its arms and legs for details.

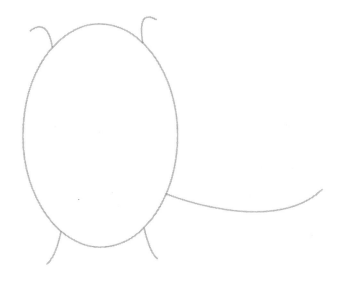

1.

First, draw a round guide for the body and lines for the legs, antennae and tail.

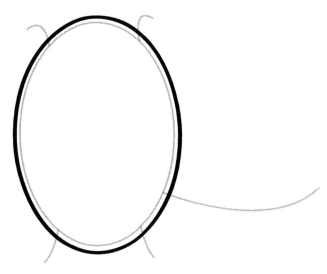

2.

Draw the body of the monster.

3.

Draw the tail and the legs of the monster.

4.

Draw the antennae of the monster.

5. Draw the eye of the monster.

6. Draw the mouth and tongue of the monster. Remove the line guides. Add four circles on its body for details.

1.

Draw two round guides for the monster's head and body. Create line guides for the arms, legs and antennae.

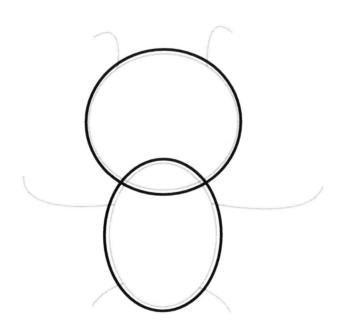

2.

Draw the outline of the monster's head and body.

3.

Draw the arms, legs and antennae

4.

Draw the eyes, nose and mouth.

5. Draw its teeth and nails.

6. Remove the line guides. Draw circles all over its body.

1.

First, draw a circle guide for the body and add line guides for the arms, legs and ears.

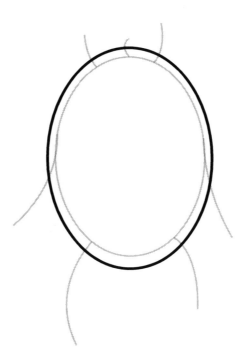

2.

Draw a circle for the body of the monster.

3.

Draw the legs of the monster.

4.

Draw the arms and ears of the monster.

5. Draw the eye and mouth.

6. Draw the teeth. Remove the line guides.
Add thin lines all over the body for details.

1.

Draw a slanting oval shaped guide for its body and add line guides for its arms and legs.

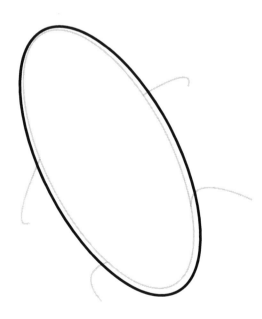

2.

Draw the body of the monster.

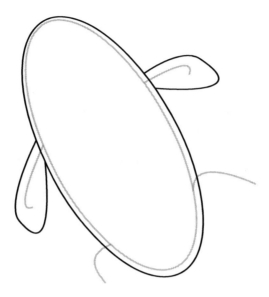

3.

Draw the arms of the monster.

4.

Draw the legs of the monster.

5.

Draw the eye and mouth of the monster.

6.

Remove the line guides. Add curvy lines for detail.

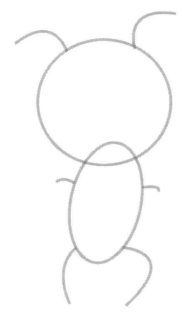

1.

First, draw two round guides for the head and body of the monster. Add line guides for the legs, arms and antennae.

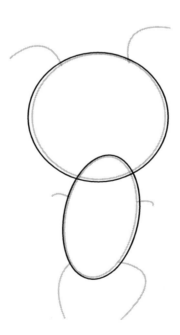

2.

Draw the outline of the head and the body of the monster.

3.

Draw the legs of the monster.

4.

Draw the antennae and little arms of the monster.

5.

Draw the eye and mouth of the monster.

6.

Remove the line guides and add short curve lines as details on its body.

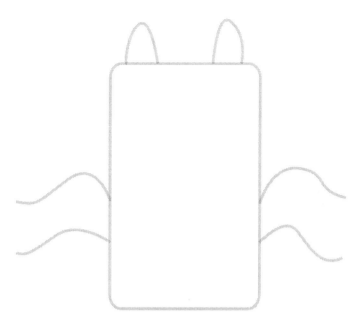

1.

Draw rectangular guide for its body. Add line guides for its tentacles and curvy lines for its ears.

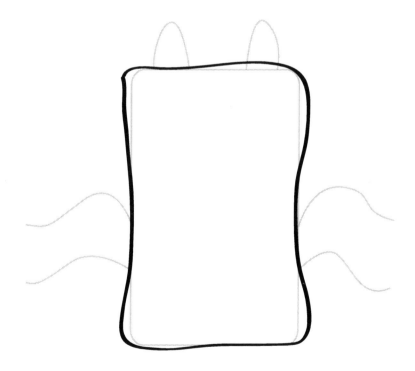

2.

Draw the body of the monster.

3.

Draw the tentacles of the monster.

4.

Draw the ears of the monster.

5.

Draw an eye, a mouth, a tongue and a tooth.

6.

Remove the line guides. Draw curvy lines on the monster to add details.

1.

First, draw a round guide for the body,
then add lines for the arms, horns and legs.

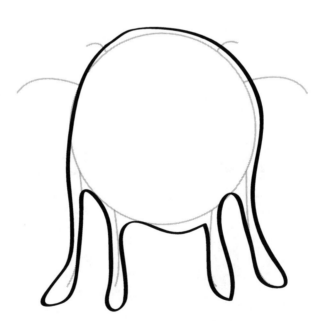

2.

Draw the body and legs of the monster.

3.

Draw the arms and claws of the monster.

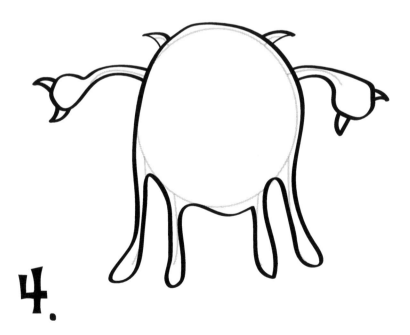

4.

Draw the horns of the monster.

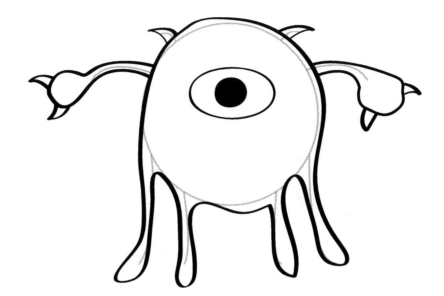

5.

Draw the eye of the monster.

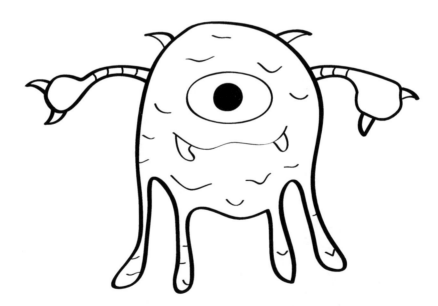

6.

Remove the line guides. Add curvy lines on the monster's body for details.

1.

First, draw a rectangular guide for the body and lines for the arms, feet and hair.

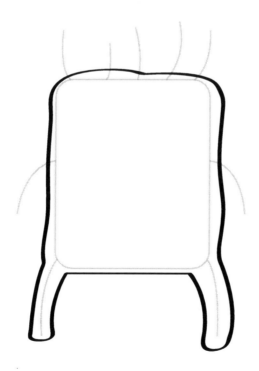

2.

Draw the body and feet of the monster.

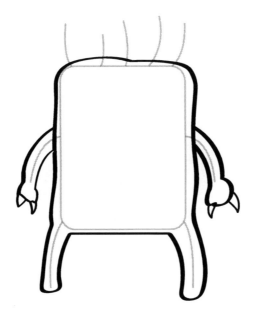

3.

Draw the arms and claws of the monster.

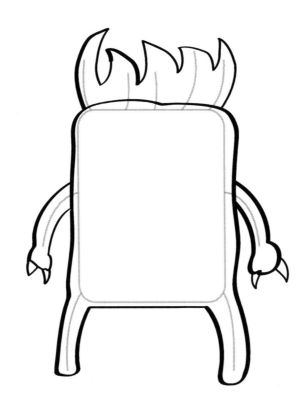

4.

Draw the hair of the monster.

5.

Draw a big eye and a small eye for the monster and add the mouth.

6.

Remove the line guides and draw curvy lines all over the body for details.

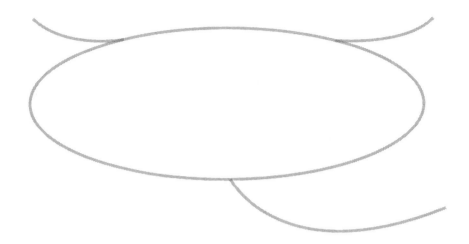

1.

First, draw an oval guide for the monster's body. Draw line guides for its wings and tail.

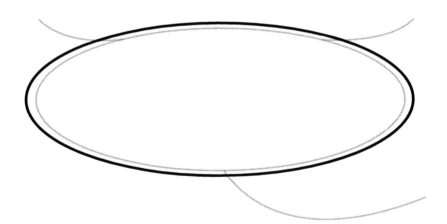

2.

Draw the outline of the body.

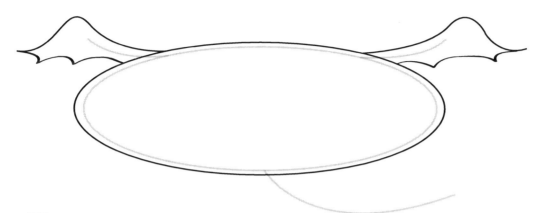

3.

Draw the wings of the monster.

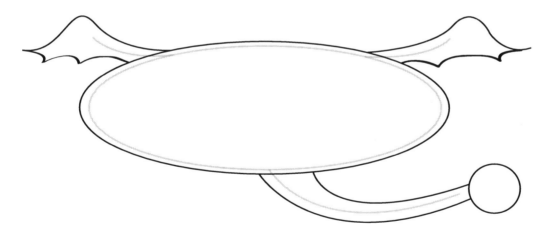

4.

Draw the tail of the monster.

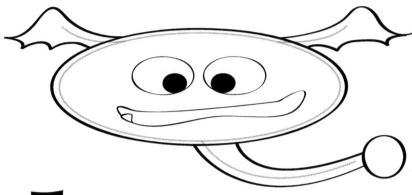

5.

Draw its two big eyes and mouth.

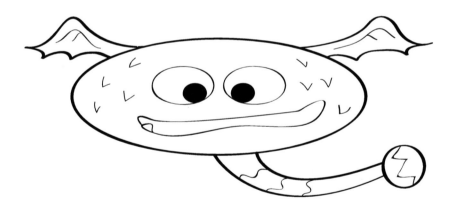

6.

Remove the line guides. Put some lines for details.

1.

First, draw line guides for its body and arms.

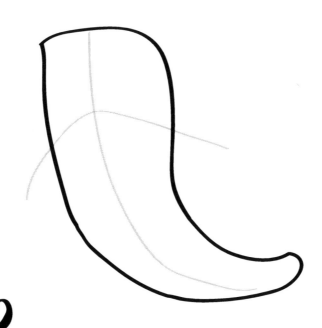

2.

Draw the outline of its body.

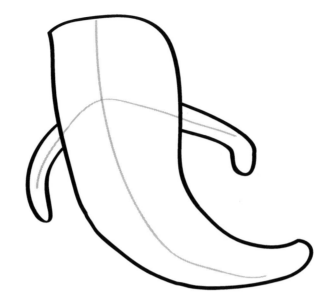

3.

Draw the arms of the monster.

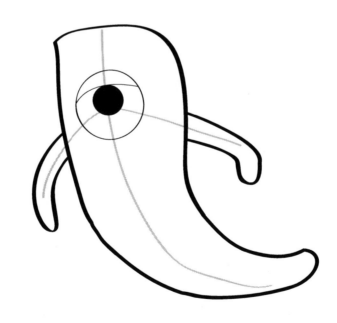

4.

Draw a big eye for the monster.

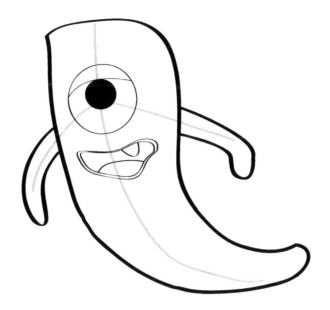

5.

Draw the mouth and tooth of the monster.

6.

Remove the line guides. Add swirly lines on its body for details.

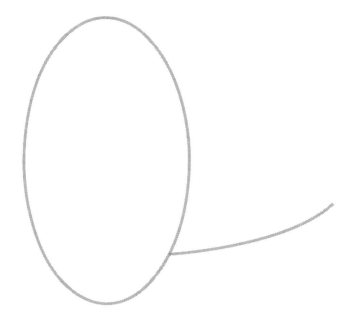

1.

First, draw a circular guide for its body.
Draw a line for its tail.

2.

Draw an outline of its body.

3.

Draw the monster's eyes.

4.

Draw the monster's tail.

5.

Draw the mouth and teeth of the monster.

6.

Remove the line guides. Add curves on its body for details.

1.

First, draw a square guide for its body and lines for its legs.

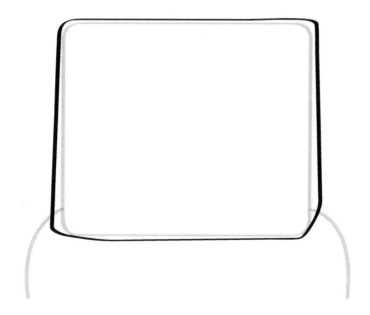

2.

Draw an outline of the monster's body.

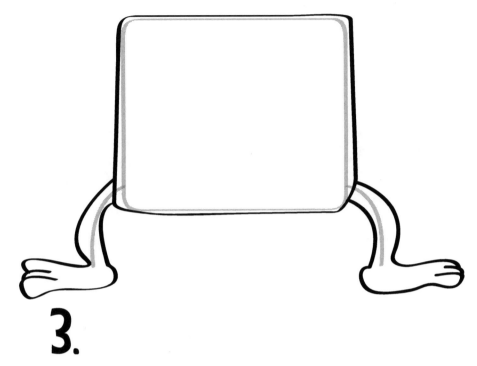

3.

Draw two legs for your monster.

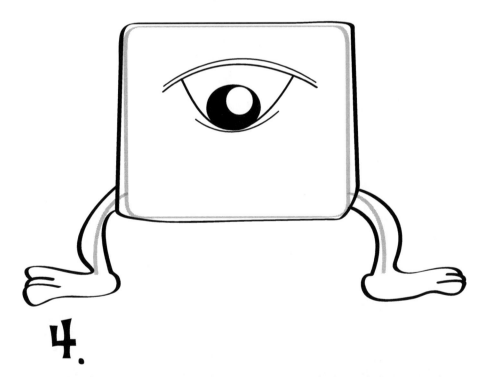

4.

Draw a huge eye on the monster.

5.

Draw the mouth, tooth and tongue of the monster.

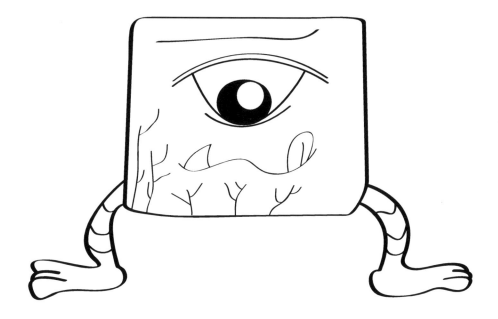

6.

Remove the line guides. Add some lines on its body for details.

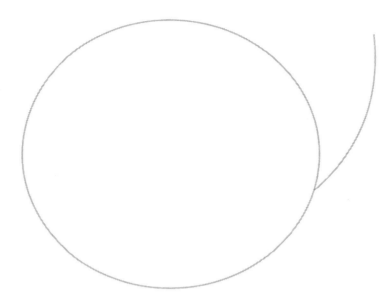

1. First, draw a huge circular guide for its body. Draw a line for the tail.

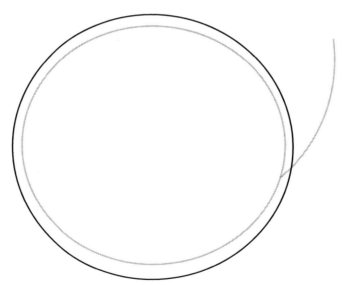

2. Draw an outline for the monster's body.

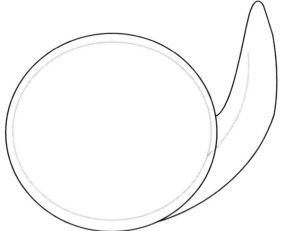

3.

Draw the tail of the monster.

4.

Draw its eyes and mouth.

5.

Draw spikes around its tail.

6.

Draw its teeth. Remove the line guides.
Add scales all over its body for details.

1.

Draw a round guide for the monster's head.
Draw line guides for the legs, arms, tail
and body.

2.

Draw the outline of the monster's head.

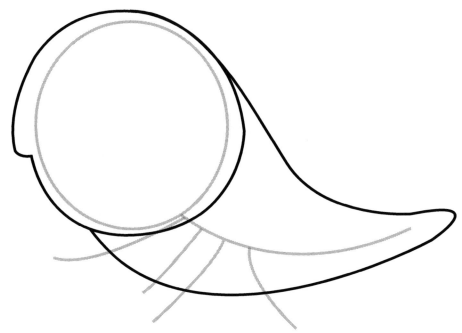

3.

Draw the outline of the monster's body down to its tail.

4.

Draw the arms and legs of the monster.

5. Draw its eyes and mouth.

6.

Draw circles on its body. Remove the line guides.

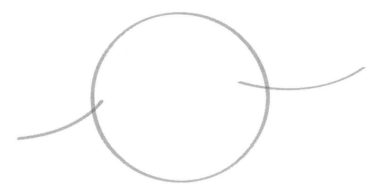

1.

First, draw a circular guide for its body and curved lines for its wings.

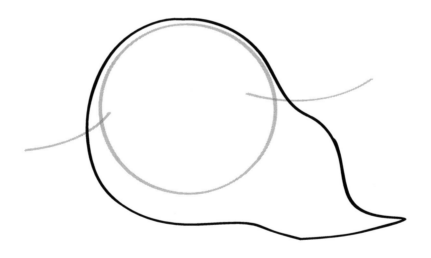

2.

Draw the body of the monster.

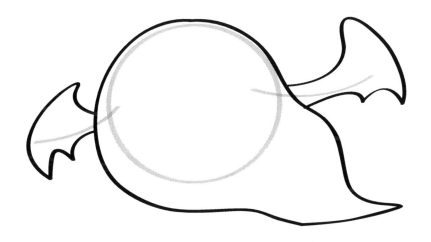

3.

Draw the monster's wings.

4.

Draw three eyes with different sizes.

5.

Draw a mouth full of sharp teeth.

6.

Remove the line guides. Add swirly lines for details.

1.

Draw two circular guides for the body and curve lines for its ears and legs.

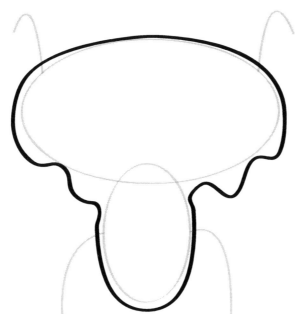

2.

Draw its body and head.

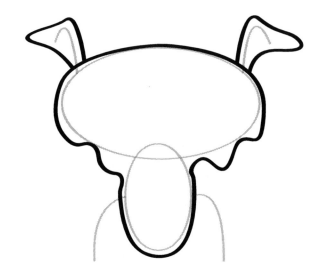

3.

Draw two large ears for the monster.

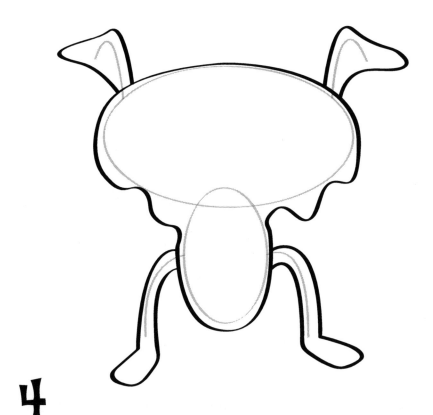

4.

Draw the monster's feet.

5.

Draw the monster's eyes and mouth.

6.

Remove the line guides. Add lines and spots on its body for details.

1.

First, draw a circular guide and lines for its body.

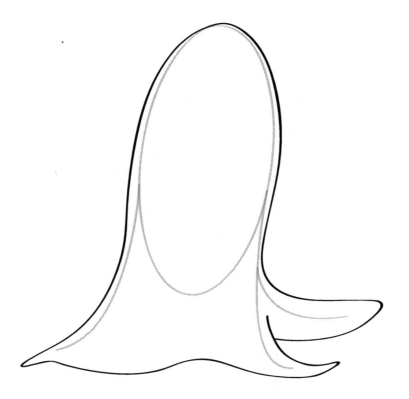

2.

Draw the monster's body.

3.

Draw a big eye on the monster's body.

4.

Draw its mouth and teeth.

5.

Draw the monster's belly.

6.

Remove line guides. Add curvy lines on its body for details.

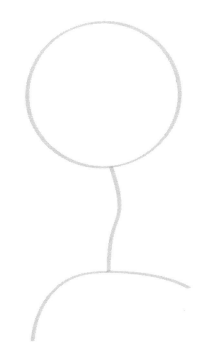

1.

First, draw a circular guide for the monster's head. Add lines for its body and feet.

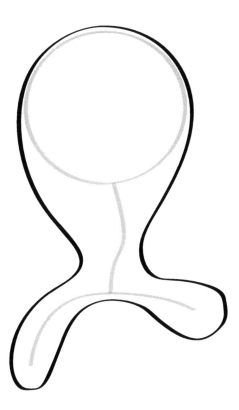

2.

Draw its head, body and feet.

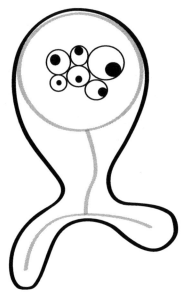

3. Draw multiple eyes on its head.

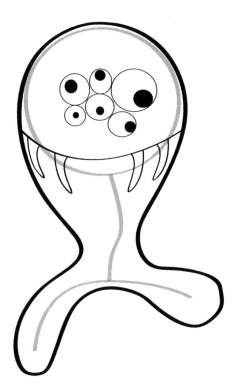

4. Draw the monster's mouth with sharp teeth.

5.

Draw claws on its feet.

6.

Remove the guides. Add lines for details.

1.

First, draw a round guide for the monster's body and lines for its arms and leg.

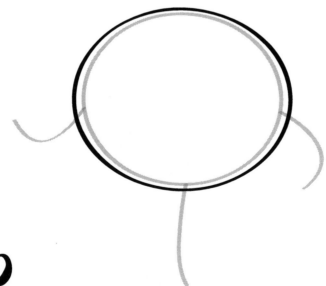

2.

Draw the monster's body.

3.

Draw the monster's two arms.

4.

Draw a leg for the monster.

5.

Draw the eyes of the monster.

6.

Remove the line guides. Add the monster's mouth, tongue and teeth. Draw a band aid over one of its eyes. Put lines for details.

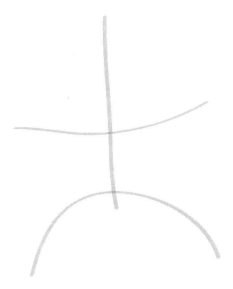

1.

First, draw line guides for the monster's body, arms and legs.

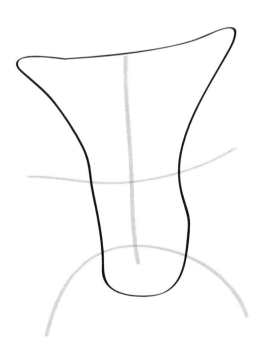

2.

Draw the body of the monster.

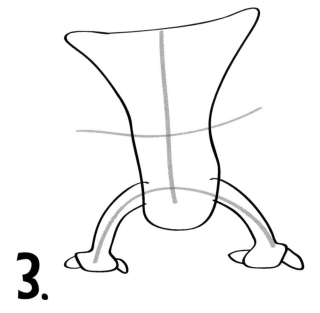

3.

Draw its legs and claws.

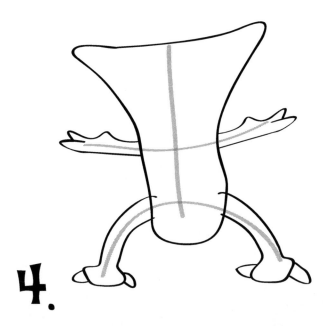

4.

Draw the arms of the monster.

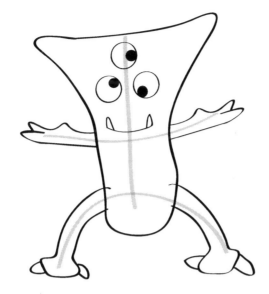

5.

Draw three eyes on its head and its mouth and teeth.

6.

Remove the line guides. Add lines on its body for details.

1.

Draw two circular guides for the monster's body. Draw lines for its arms and feet.

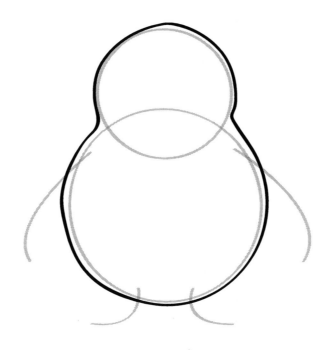

2.

Draw an outline of the monster's body.

3.

Draw the monster's hairy feet.

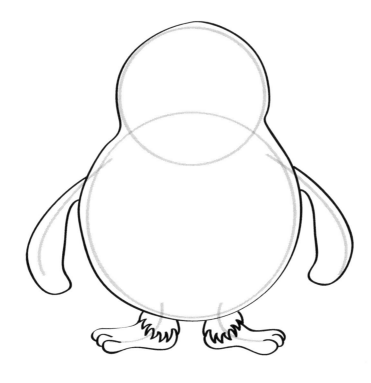

4.

Draw the arms of the monster.

5.

Draw 2 large eyes for the monster. Add the
mouth and teeth.

6.

Add spots on its body for details. Remove
the line guides.

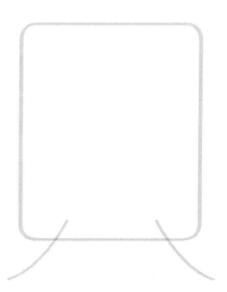

1.

Draw a rectangular guide for the monster's body.
Add lines for its feet.

2.

Draw the outline of the monster's body.

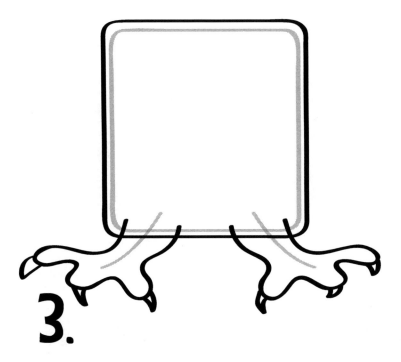

3.

Draw its feet with claws.

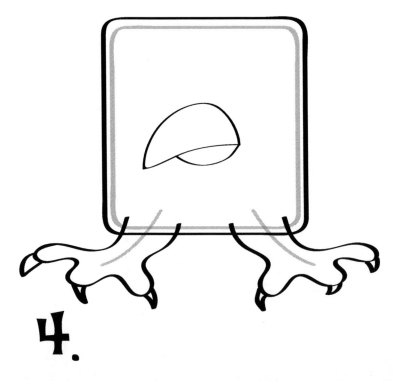

4.

Draw the monster's beak.

5.

Draw the eyes of the monster.

6.

Remove the line guides. Put swirly and curvy lines to add details.

1.

Draw a round guide for the monster's body. Add lines for its legs, horn and tail.

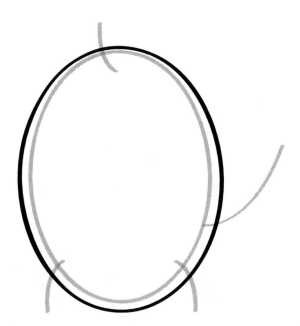

2.

Draw the outline of the monster's body.

3.

Draw the monster's feet and horn.

4.

Draw the monster's tail

5.
Draw the monster's mouth and teeth.
Draw an eye inside the monster's mouth.

6.
Remove line guides. Add lines on its horn
and triangular spots on its body for details.

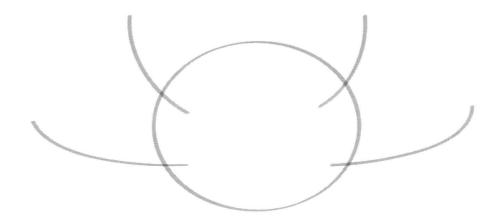

1. First, draw a cirle for the monster's body. Add lines for its eyes and wings.

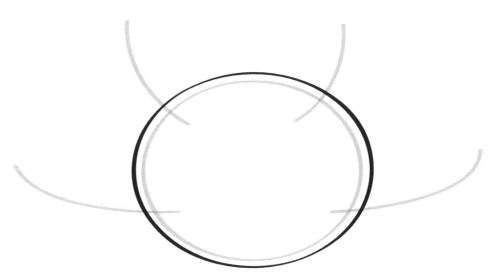

2. Draw an outline of its body.

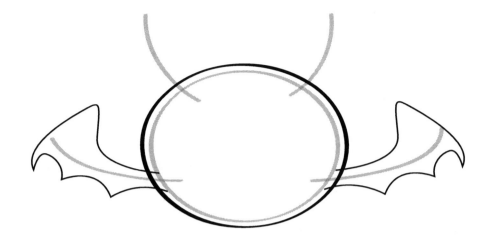

3.

Draw a pair of wings on its side.

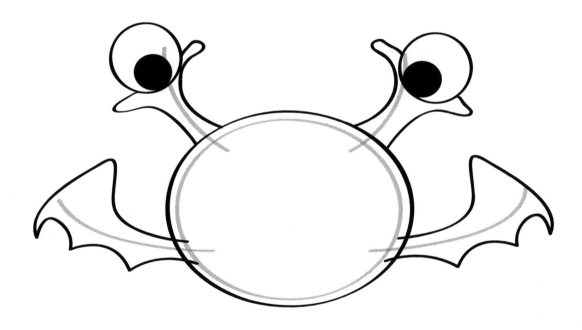

4.

Draw the monster's eyes and tubes to connect the monster's eyes to its body.

5.

Draw a huge mouth with its teeth and tongue.

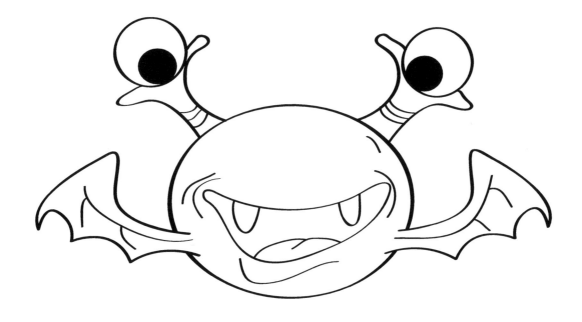

6.

Remove line guides. Add lines on the monster's body for details.

Made in the USA
Lexington, KY
13 February 2018